Novels for Students, Volume 3 Copyright Notice

Since this page cannot legibly accommodate all copyright notices, the acknowledgments constitute an extension of the copyright notice.

While every effort has been made to secure permission to reprint material and to ensure the reliability of the information presented in this publication, Gale Research neither guarantees the accuracy of the data contained herein nor assumes any responsibility for errors, omissions, or discrepancies. Gale accepts no payment for listing; and inclusion in the publication of any organization, agency, institution, publication, service, or individual does not imply endorsement of the editors or publisher. Errors brought to the attention of the publisher and verified to the satisfaction of the publisher will be corrected in future editions.

This publication is a creative work fully protected

by all applicable copyright laws, as well as by misappropriation, trade secret, unfair competition, and other applicable laws. The authors and editors of this work have added value to the underlying factual material herein through one or more of the following: unique and original selection, coordination, expression, arrangement, and classification of the information. All rights to this publication will be vigorously defended.

Copyright © 1998

Gale Research
835 Penobscot Building
645 Griswold St.
Detroit, MI 48226-4094

All rights reserved including the right of reproduction in whole or in part in any form.

This book is printed on acid-free paper that meets the minimum requirements of American National Standard for Information Sciences—Permanence Paper for Printed Library Materials, ANSI Z39.48-1984.

ISBN 0-7876-2113-7
ISSN 1094-3552

Printed in the United States of America.
10 9 8 7 6 5 4

A Passage to India

E. M. Forster
1924

Introduction

A Passage to India, published in 1924, was E. M. Forster's first novel in fourteen years, and the last novel he wrote. Subtle and rich in symbolism, the novel works on several levels. On the surface, it is about India—which at the time was a colonial possession of Britain—and about the relations between British and Indian people in that country. It is also about the necessity of friendship, and about the difficulty of establishing friendship across cultural boundaries. On a more symbolic level, the novel also addresses questions of faith (both religious faith and faith in social conventions). Forster's narrative centers on Dr. Aziz, a young Indian physician whose attempt to establish friendships with several British characters has disastrous consequences. In the course of the novel, Dr. Aziz is accused of attempting to rape a young Englishwoman. Aziz's friend Mr. Fielding, a British teacher, helps to defend Aziz. Although the charges against Aziz are dropped during his trial, the gulf between the British and native Indians grows wider than ever, and the novel ends on an ambiguous note. When *A Passage to India* appeared in 1924, it was praised by reviewers in a number of important British and American literary journals. Despite some criticism that Forster had depicted the British unfairly, the book was popular with readers in both Britain and the United States. The year after its publication, the novel received two prestigious literary awards—the James Tait Black Memorial Prize and the Prix Femina Vie Heureuse. More than seventy years later, it remains highly regarded. Not only do many scholars, critics, and other writers consider it a classic of early twentieth-century fiction, but in a survey of readers conducted by Waterstone's Bookstore and Channel 4 television in Britain at the end of 1996, it was voted as one of the "100 Greatest Books of the Century."

Author Biography

When Edward Morgan Forster completed *A Passage to India*, he was in his mid-forties and was already a respected and relatively successful novelist. Between 1905 and 1910 he had published four well-crafted Edwardian novels of upper-middle class life and manners: *Where Angels Fear to Tread* (1905), *The Longest Journey* (1907), *A Room With a View* (1908), and *Howards End* (1910). However, although he had continued to write short stories as well as another novel, *Maurice* (published in 1971, after Forster's death), he published little in the decade after *Howards End.*

Born in London on January 1, 1879, E. M. Forster was an only child. His father, an architect, died when Forster was only a year old. The boy was raised by his mother, grandmother, and his father's aunt, who left Forster the sum of 8,000 pounds in her will. This large amount of money eventually paid for Forster's education and his early travels. Early in the new twentieth century it also enabled him to live independently while he established his career as a writer.

Forster grew up in the English countryside north of London, where he had a happy early childhood. He attended an Eastbourne preparatory school and then the family moved to Kent so that he could attend Tonbridge School (a traditional English public school), where he was miserable.

However, he found happiness and intellectual stimulation when he went to Cambridge University. There, at King's College, he studied the classics and joined a student intellectual society known as the Apostles. Among his teachers was the philosopher G. E. Moore, who had an important influence on Forster's views. He made many friends and acquaintances, some of whom went on to become important writers and eventually became active in the Bloomsbury Group.

After graduating from Cambridge, Forster traveled in Italy and Greece. These experiences further broadened his outlook, and he decided to become a writer. He became an instructor at London's Working Men's College in 1902 and remained with them for two decades.

In 1906, while living with his mother in the town of Weybridge, near London, Forster tutored an Indian student named Syed Ross Masood. The two developed a close friendship, and Forster became curious about India. In 1912 Forster visited India for the first time, with some friends from Cambridge University, and spent some time with Masood there. He stayed in India for six months and saw the town of Bankipore, located on the Ganges River in northeast India. Bankipore became the model for Chandrapore. Forster also saw the nearby Barabar Caves, which gave him the idea for the Marabar Caves. While in India he wrote first drafts of seven chapters of a new novel that would become *A Passage to India.* However, after returning to England he put the work aside and instead wrote

Maurice, a novel about a homosexual love affair. Because its theme was considered very controversial at the time, Forster decided not to publish this book during his lifetime.

During World War I, Forster worked as a Red Cross volunteer in Alexandria, Egypt. In 1921 he made a second visit to India, where he spent six months as private secretary to the Maharajah of Dewas Senior, an independent Moslem state. He gathered more material about India, and after returning to England he finished writing *A Passage to India*, which he dedicated to Masood. Forster found the writing process difficult and feared that the book would be a failure. He was relieved by the book's favorable reception, and in the remaining forty-five years of his life he received many awards and honors. Although he continued to write short stories, essays, and radio programs, he turned away from the novel form.

Forster died of a stroke on June 7, 1970, in Coventry, England. Today, his literary reputation remains high, and all of his novels, except *The Longest Journey*, have been adapted into films.

Plot Summary

Part I—Mosque

Set in India several decades before the end of British Rule, *A Passage to India* by E. M. Forster explores the relationships that ensue when Dr. Aziz, an Indian doctor, is befriended by Mrs. Moore and Miss Adela Quested, two recently arrived Englishwomen. In the opening scene, Dr. Aziz is involved in a discussion about whether or not it is possible for an Indian to be friends with an Englishman. The conversation is interrupted by a message from the Civil Surgeon, Major Callendar, who requests Dr. Aziz's immediate assistance. Aziz makes his way to Callendar's compound but arrives only to be told that the Civil Surgeon is out. On his way back home, Aziz stops in a mosque to rest and meets Mrs. Moore. He is delighted by her kind behavior and accompanies her back to the Chandrapore Club. Mrs. Moore's son, City Magistrate Ronny Heaslop, quickly learns of his mother's meeting with the Indian doctor. He instructs her not to mention the incident to his fiancee, Miss Quested, because he does not want her wondering whether the "natives" are treated properly "and all that sort of nonsense."

Meanwhile, Adela, who travelled all the way from England to decide whether or not she will marry Ronny, expresses her desire "to see the real

India." The Collector, Mr. Turton, makes plans to throw a Bridge Party—a party to bridge the gulf between East and West. But the event is not a great success and Adela thinks her countrymen mad for inviting guests and then not receiving them amiably. One of the few officials who does make a genuine effort to make the party work is Mr. Fielding, the Principal of the Government College. He hosts a gathering of his own a couple of days later, and it is then that Dr. Aziz first meets Adela and invites her and Mrs. Moore to visit the nearby Marabar Caves. It is also on this afternoon that a friendship begins to develop between Aziz and Fielding.

Part II—Caves

The day of the visit to the Marabar Caves arrives and, except for the absence of Fielding and his assistant, Professor Godbole, who miss the early morning train, the expedition begins successfully. An elephant transports the party into the hills and a picnic breakfast awaits Aziz's guests when they reach their goal near the caves. However, things begin to change when they visit the first cave. Mrs. Moore nearly faints when she feels herself crammed in the dark and loses sight of Adela and Dr. Aziz. She feels something strike her face and hears a terrifying echo:

> The echo in a Marabar cave is … entirely devoid of distinction. Whatever is said, the same monotonous noise replies, and

> quivers up and down the walls until it is absorbed into the roof. 'Boum' is the sound as far as the human alphabet can express it, or 'bououm', or 'ou-boum,'—utterly dull. Hope, politeness, the blowing of a nose, the squeak of a boot, all produce 'boum'.... Coming at a moment when [Mrs. Moore] chanced to be fatigued, it had managed to murmur: 'Pathos, piety, courage—they exist, but are identical, and so is filth. Everything exists, nothing has value.' If one had spoken vileness in that place, or quoted lofty poetry, the comment would have been the same—'ou-boum.'

The echo lingers in Mrs. Moore's mind and begins "in some indescribable way to undermine her hold on life." She suddenly realizes that she no longer wants to communicate with her children, Aziz, God, or anyone else and sinks into a state of apathy and cynicism.

Meanwhile, Aziz and Adela are en route to visit more of the caves. Preoccupied by thoughts of her marriage and by the disturbing realization that she and Ronny do not love each other, Adela inadvertently offends her host by asking an ill-thought question. Aziz is momentarily annoyed and slips into one of the caves "to recover his balance." Adela loses sight of him and also enters one of the caves. When Aziz reappears, he catches a glimpse of Adela running down the hill towards an approaching car. Thinking that she has merely gone off to meet Ronny, Aziz returns to the camp and learns that Adela has unexpectedly driven away. The remaining members of the expedition take the train back to Chandrapore. Upon their return, Dr. Aziz is arrested and charged with making insulting advances to Miss Quested in the Marabar Caves.

That evening, there is a meeting at the Club and Fielding stands alone against his countrymen by stating his belief that Aziz is innocent. Adela remains ill for several days, hovering "between common sense and hysteria" and, like Mrs. Moore, is plagued by the sound of the echo. She begins to have doubts about what happened in the cave and eventually tells Ronny that she may have made a mistake. Mrs. Moore supports Adela's belief that Aziz is innocent but Ronny insists that the trial must proceed and sends his mother back to England. When Adela takes the stand, she feels herself returned to the Marabar Hills and finds the exact reply to all the questions put to her. However, she is unable to say for sure whether Aziz followed her into the cave; she could see herself in one of the caves, but could not locate Aziz. Finally she tells the court that she has made a mistake and that Dr. Aziz never followed her into the cave. The Superintendent withdraws the charges and Aziz is released "without one stain on his character."

After the trial, Adela receives the news of Mrs. Moore's death at sea and can no longer bear Ronny's company. He eventually breaks off their engagement because marrying her would now ruin his career. Before her voyage back to England, Adela is subjected to one final adventure when her servant, Antony, attempts to blackmail her by claiming she was Fielding's mistress. By this time, Fielding, who believes that Adela should not suffer for her mistake, has managed to convince Aziz to renounce his right to monetary compensation. Aziz begins to regret that decision when he hears the "naughty rumour" concerning his two friends. The misunderstanding is complicated when Aziz learns that Fielding is also returning to England. Aziz suspects that his friend intends to marry Adela for her money and leaves Chandrapore before Fielding can explain or say good-bye.

Part III—Temple

Two years later, Dr. Aziz and Professor Godbole are both living in Mau, a town several hundred miles west of the Marabar Hills and which is currently in the midst of Hindu religious celebrations. Dr. Aziz has learned that Fielding, along with his wife and brother-in-law, will soon be stopping in Mau on business. Fielding had sent his old friend a letter explaining all the details about his wedding to Stella Moore, Mrs. Moore's daughter, but Aziz never read it. As a result, he still thinks that Fielding has married Adela. All misunderstandings are finally cleared up when they meet, but Aziz does not care who Fielding has married; his heart is now with his own people and he wishes no Englishman or Englishwoman to be his friend.

Later that day, Fielding and his wife borrow a boat in order to watch the religious procession. Aziz runs into Ralph Moore and brings him out on the water too, thereby repeating the gesture of hospitality he had intended to make through the visit to the Marabar Caves two years earlier. At the height of the ceremony, the two boats collide and all are thrown into the water. The accident erases all bitterness between Fielding and Aziz and the two go back "laughingly to their old relationship." A few days later, they go for a ride in the Mau jungles and Aziz gives Fielding a letter for Miss Quested in which he thanks her for her fine behavior two years back. They talk about politics and Aziz foresees the day when India shall finally get rid of the English. Then, Aziz tells Fielding, "you and I shall be friends."

Characters

Mahmoud Ali

A close friend of Dr. Aziz. A Moslem and a lawyer, he is often in the company of Aziz and Hamidullah. In Chapter II, Mahmoud Ali declares that it is not possible for Indians to be friends with the English; Hamidullah argues that such friendship is possible. Mahmoud Ali is generally cynical, and he often makes sharp comments about other characters. He helps to defend Aziz at Aziz's trial.

Mr. Amritrao

A famous Hindu barrister (trial lawyer) from Calcutta who is hired to defend Dr. Aziz at his trial. Mr. Amritrao, reputed to be one of the finest Indian lawyers in the country, has made his name as a radical who is "notoriously anti-British." His hiring causes some controversy, and the move is regarded as a political challenge to the British. During the trial, Amritrao objects to the fact that Adela's British supporters have been allowed to sit on a platform at the front of the courtroom, and they are forced to move.

Dr. Aziz

A young doctor who is the central Indian

character in the novel. Dr. Aziz is a Moslem and a widower. His three children live with his wife's mother. He is described as "an athletic little man, daintily put together but really very strong." He works at the government hospital in Chandrapore, under the supervision of Major Callendar. In addition to his practical skill as a doctor, he also has a romantic side and writes poetry. His favorite poetic themes are "the decay of Islam and the brevity of Love." Although he is thoroughly Indian, he idealizes the cultures of Persia and Arabia, where the Islamic faith originated. He regards the historical Mogul emperors of India as his models. In the early part of the novel he is disdainful of Hindus; although they are Indians, he considers them foreign. Because of his good education and respected professional situation, Aziz believes that he can be accepted by the British as almost their equal. Despite a melancholy streak, Aziz possesses a sense of humor, and hospitality is important to him. He is eager to please and impress people whom he considers kind and thoughtful, and early in the novel he especially wants to make friends with Mrs. Moore and Mr. Fielding. However, his very goodwill and his somewhat impulsive nature get him into situations that cause him trouble. ("Aziz overrated hospitality, mistaking it for intimacy, and not seeing that it is tainted with the sense of possession.") He at first wants to invite Mrs. Moore and Fielding to his house, but then realizes that this is not a suitable place for entertaining Western guests. On the spur of the moment, he asks Mrs. Moore, Fielding, and Adela

Quested to join him for a picnic at the Marabar Caves, a famous natural landmark outside the town. The picnic results in disaster, however, when Adela believes that Aziz has attacked her in one of the caves. He is brought to trial in Chandrapore. Although Adela drops the charges during the trial and Aziz is freed, his reputation is ruined. He becomes completely disillusioned with his position in life and develops a hatred of the British. In Part III of the novel, he has moved to the Hindu state of Mau and given up his medical ambitions; instead, he is content to be a simple "medicine man" to the state's ailing ruler. At the end of the book he is reconciled with his British friend Fielding but tells him that they can only be true friends after the British have left India.

Nawab Bahadur

A distinguished Moslem who is a leading figure in the Indian community in the Chandrapore district. ("Nawab" is an honorary title.) The Nawab Bahadur is an older man, "a big proprietor and a philanthropist, a man of benevolence and decision." A supporter of British rule in India, he is also known for his hospitality and loyalty to his friends. Ronny Heaslop and Adela Quested are riding in the Nawab's car when it runs off the road. Following the incident at the Marabar Caves, the Nawab proclaims Dr. Aziz's innocence and attends his trial. After the trial he renounces his title and is known simply by his original name, Mr. Zulfiqar. A victory banquet is held at his mansion, where Aziz,

Fielding, and Hamidullah lie on the roof and discuss the trial and its consequences.

Major Callendar

The head of the government hospital in Chandrapore and a figure of some authority in the Anglo-Indian (British) community. Major Callendar holds the post of civil surgeon and is Dr. Aziz's immediate superior at the hospital. The most arrogant of the British officials in Chandrapore, he is "dour," gruff, and plain-spoken to the point of offensiveness. In Chapter II he summons Dr. Aziz to his bungalow, interrupting Aziz's pleasant evening with his friends. When Aziz arrives after a short delay, a servant informs him that Callendar is not at home and has not left a message. After Aziz's aborted trial, Callendar makes some intemperate remarks about Indians at the club, where the members of the Anglo-Indian community have gathered. We later learn that Callendar has been replaced as civil surgeon by a Major Roberts.

Media Adaptations

- *A Passage to India* was adapted as a film by David Lean, starring Judy Davis, Victor Banerjee, Peggy Ashcroft, James Fox, and Alec Guinness, Columbia, 1984. It was nominated for eleven Academy Awards, including Best Picture; Ashcroft was named Best Supporting Actress for her portrayal of Mrs. Moore. Available from Columbia Tristar Home Video.

- *A Passage to India* was adapted for the stage by Santha Rama Ran, produced in London, 1960, produced on Broadway, 1962; adapted for television by John Maynard, BBC-TV, 1968.

Collector

See Mr. Turton

Mr. Das

The assistant magistrate (judge) in Chandrapore and thus the assistant to Ronny Heaslop, the magistrate. Das, a Hindu, presides over the trial of Dr. Aziz. (Ronny has excused himself from sitting on the case because of his relationship with Adela Quested, who has brought the charges against Aziz.) Ronny expresses confidence in Das's ability to conduct an orderly trial, but Major Callendar declares that Das is not trustworthy because he is an Indian. Das follows correct procedures in the trial and does not show favoritism toward either the prosecution or the defense. After the trial Das visits Dr. Aziz for medical treatment and also requests a poem from Aziz for his brother-in-law's magazine. Das's friendly visit represents a new spirit of cooperation between the Moslem and Hindu communities.

Miss Nancy Derek

An unconventional Englishwoman. Young and single, Miss Derek is regarded with some distrust by the British community at Chandrapore because of her unorthodox behavior. She is not part of the civil station at Chandrapore, but serves as a personal assistant to the Maharani of Mudkul, an independent Indian state. When Adela Quested and

Ronny Heaslop are in a minor car accident, Miss Derek comes along and drives them back to Chandrapore. She again shows up in her car near the Marabar Caves as Adela is running from the caves and drives Adela back to Chandrapore. After Dr. Aziz's trial, Aziz and Fielding discuss a rumor that Miss Derek is having an affair with Mr. McBryde, the Superintendent of Police.

Mr. Cyril Fielding

The principal of the Government College (that is, a British-run school) in Chandrapore. Fielding develops a close friendship with Dr. Aziz during the course of the novel and is the only Englishman to publicly express his belief in Aziz's innocence. In contrast to such Anglo-Indian (British) career administrators as Mr. Turton and Major Callendar, Fielding arrived in India relatively late in his life—after the age of forty. By the time he arrives in India, he has already had a "varied career." He is described as "a hard-bitten, good-tempered, intelligent fellow on the verge of middle age, with a belief in education." Because of his more easygoing and broadminded attitudes, he is regarded with some suspicion by his fellow expatriates, especially the women. Indeed, he has no particular enthusiasm for the conventional social life of Chandrapore's Anglo-Indian community, and thus "the gulf between himself and his countrymen ... widened distressingly." Moreover, he has "no racial feeling"—he regards Indians simply as people from another country, not as inferiors. He believes that people from different parts of the world can understand one another "by the help of good will plus culture and intelligence." He is "happiest in the give-and-take of private conversation." This emphasis on the importance of friendship and the personal over the professional life makes Fielding a representative of Forster's own views. In Chapter VII, Fielding gives a tea party attended by Aziz, Mrs. Moore, Adela Quested, and Professor Godbole (who teaches at the college). The party is a success, bringing together Christian, Moslem, and Hindu as equals. However, the party sets in motion the disastrous events of the excursion to the Marabar Caves. Fielding is supposed to travel to the caves with Aziz and the English women, but he misses the train. When Adela returns to Chandrapore with Miss Derek and claims that Aziz has attempted to rape her, Fielding goes to see Inspector McBryde. Fielding tells McBryde that there has been some misunderstanding and that Aziz is innocent, but McBryde becomes angry at Fielding's interference. Because he supports Aziz and insults Ronny Heaslop, Fielding is forced to resign from the English club in Chandrapore. Adela stays with Fielding after the trial. Fielding has a long conversation with Aziz at the post-trial victory party at the Nawab Bahadur's house, but their friendship cools. Fielding soon returns to England, and Aziz believes that he has married Adela. The friendship is revived somewhat when Fielding eventually returns to India with his new wife, Stella, the daughter of Mrs. Moore. However, Aziz tells Fielding that they cannot be true friends until the

British have left India, and the novel concludes on this ambiguous note.

Narayan Godbole

See Professor Godbole

Professor Godbole

An Indian who teaches at the college in Chandrapore, where Mr. Fielding is the principal. He is a friend of Dr. Aziz. Godbole is a Hindu (of the Brahmin caste, the highest caste in the Hindu religion) and remains somewhat aloof. Godbole is supposed to take part in the trip to the Marabar Caves organized by Aziz. However, he and Fielding miss the train on which Aziz, Mrs. Moore, and Adela Quested are traveling because Godbole takes too much time saying his prayers before leaving for the station. In the third part of the novel, "Temple," Professor Godbole has moved to the Hindu state of Mau, where he is Minister of Education in the local government. Godbole is the central symbolic figure in this part of the book, representing the Hindu philosophy of acceptance. Ironically, he may also be more representative of the "real" India than is Aziz. He takes part in the ceremony held to celebrate the rebirth of the Hindu god Krishna.

Hamidullah

A Moslem Indian who is a good friend of Dr. Aziz. He was educated at Cambridge University in

England and is "the leading barrister [trial lawyer] of Chandrapore." In chapter two, Hamidullah, Aziz, and Mahmoud Ali discuss whether it is possible for an Indian to be friends with the British. Hamidullah recounts his own experience in England some years earlier. He had been welcomed into the home of an English couple, whom he recalls with great affection. Hamidullah helps to organize Dr. Aziz's defense after Aziz is charged with having assaulted Adela Quested in the Marabar Caves.

Ronny Heaslop

A young Anglo-Indian (British) civil servant who is the city magistrate of Chandrapore. He is the son of Mrs. Moore by her first husband. At the outset of the novel, Ronny is expected to marry Adela Quested, whom he had originally met in England. Educated in an English public (the equivalent of an American private) school, Ronny embodies a narrow, rigid concept of duty and represses the personal side of his life. He expresses the view that the Indians are not capable of governing themselves, and that Britain rules India for India's own good. When his mother and Adela arrive in India, they are disappointed to find that Ronny has changed. Adela perceives that "India had developed sides of his character that she had never admired," such as "self-complacency," "censoriousness," and "lack of subtlety." She also finds that "when proved wrong, he was particularly exasperating." Ronny disapproves of his mother's and Adela's attempts to see "the real India" and to mix with Indians socially. He becomes impatient with what he considers their naive attitude toward India. According to Ronny, "No one can even begin to know [India] until he has been in it twenty years." The alleged attempted rape of Adela at the Marabar Caves and her subsequent withdrawal of the charges against Aziz during the trial cause Ronny much embarrassment, and he breaks off their engagement.

Dr. Panna Lal

A colleague of Dr. Aziz at the government hospital in Chandrapore. A Hindu, he is described as "timid and elderly" and "of low extraction." Dr. Aziz regards Dr. Lal as "Major Callendar's spy," and he and his friends make Lal the butt of some humor. Dr. Lal urges Aziz to go with him to the Turton's Bridge Party, but at the last minute Aziz decides not to go. In Chapter VI, Dr. Lal meets Aziz and asks why he was not at the party; Aziz makes up the excuse that he had to go to the post office. In Chapter IX, Dr. Lal goes to Aziz's bungalow to treat him for a mild illness.

Mohammed Latif

A poor distant relation of Hamidullah. He is described as "a gentle, happy, and dishonest old man" who "had never done a stroke of work." Mohammed Latif serves Dr. Aziz as a general servant and dogsbody. He is often present in the book but never speaks unless he is spoken to. He accompanies Aziz, Mrs. Moore, and Adela Quested on their picnic to the Marabar Caves. In the last section, "Temple," he has left Chandrapore with Aziz and settled in Mau.

Mr. McBryde

The district superintendent of police in Chandrapore. McBryde formally arrests Dr. Aziz after Adela Quested reports the incident in the Marabar Caves. Forster describes McBryde as "the most reflective and best educated of the Chandrapore officials." He was born in India (in the town of Karachi, in present-day Pakistan), not in Britain, and he has "read and thought a good deal." His experiences, including an unhappy marriage, have made him cynical; but unlike Major Callendar, he is not a bully. He is personally sympathetic toward Aziz and acts against him out of his professional duty, not out of malice. McBryde gets angry at Fielding when Fielding tries to tell him that Aziz is innocent. He acts as the prosecutor at Aziz's trial. Aziz and Fielding later hear that McBryde has been having an affair with Miss Derek and is divorcing his wife.

Mrs. Moore

An Englishwoman who is a central figure in the book. She is the most sensitive and reflective of the English characters. An elderly widow, she is the mother of Ronny Heaslop, the Chandrapore city magistrate, by her first marriage. She also has another son, Ralph, and a daughter, Stella, by her second marriage. Mrs. Moore has recently arrived in India with Adela Quested, who is expected to marry Ronny. Mrs. Moore is introduced in Chapter II when she encounters Dr. Aziz in the mosque in Chandrapore. Dr. Aziz has gone into the mosque after his unsuccessful attempt to find Major Callendar and is startled when he discovers that a stranger—an Englishwoman—is also there. The two talk, and a friendship develops: Aziz is happy to have met an English person who is sympathetic toward him and India, while Mrs. Moore finds Aziz charming, intelligent, and interesting. (Adela Quested later tells Aziz that Mrs. Moore "learnt more about India in those few minutes' talk with you than in the three weeks since we landed.") Uncomfortable in what she considers the superficial company of the English expatriate community, Mrs. Moore decides that she wants to see "the real India." Her plans to visit two Indian women are unsuccessful, but she enjoys Mr. Fielding's tea party. At the tea party, Aziz invites Mrs. Moore, Adela, Fielding, and Professor Godbole to join him on an excursion to the Marabar Caves. (At the tea party Mrs. Moore also discusses "mysteries and muddles"; these words take on a special significance in the book.) In the meantime, Mrs. Moore quarrels with Ronny, who she finds has become narrow-minded during his time in India. When it becomes clear that Ronny and Adela will not marry, Mrs. Moore realizes that "My duties here are evidently finished. I don't want to see India now; now for my passage back." By the time of their visit to the caves, Mrs. Moore has lost interest in the trip. Tired by the heat, she finds the caves "a horrid, stuffy place," hits her head, and nearly faints. Moreover, she is alarmed by "a terrifying echo." When she emerges from the cave "the echo began in some indescribable way to undermine her hold on life." For her, the echo's message is "Everything exists, nothing has value." Shortly thereafter—just before Aziz's trial—she leaves India; we later learn that she has died on the voyage back to England. However, her presence continues to be felt after her death. Although Dr. Aziz's career is ruined by Adela's false charge of rape and he develops a hatred of the English, Aziz continues to think fondly of Mrs. Moore. Indeed, on his acquittal, the Indian crowd acclaims her as "Esmiss Esmoor," transforming her into a Hindu goddess. (The Indians apparently believe that she had somehow intervened to testify on Aziz's behalf, and regard her as a deity of justice.) At the end of the novel, the spirit of Mrs. Moore returns to India symbolically in the form of her daughter Stella, who has married Cyril Fielding.

Ralph Moore

The son of Mrs. Moore by her second husband. He is thus the brother of Stella and half-brother of Ronny Heaslop. Ralph is mentioned several times in the book but does not appear until near the end of the novel, when he arrives in Mau with his sister Stella and her new husband, Cyril Fielding. Dr. Aziz meets Ralph and treats his bee stings.

Stella Moore

Mrs. Moore's daughter. Stella's father was Mrs. Moore's second husband; she is thus the full sister of Ralph and the half-sister of Ronny Heaslop. Stella is mentioned by Mrs. Moore and referred to at several points in the novel. She lives in England and does not actually appear until the end of the novel, when she arrives in the Hindu native state of Mau with Ralph and with her new husband, Cyril Fielding. Dr. Aziz had mistakenly assumed that Fielding had married Adela Quested. Aziz is surprised and pleased when he learns that Stella, not Adela, is Fielding's wife. However, Aziz's attitude toward Stella is ambiguous because she is related both to Mrs. Moore, whom Aziz had admired, and to Ronny, whom he dislikes. Fielding confides that Stella "has ideas I don't share…. My wife's after something." This suggests that she has a deeper understanding of life than either Aziz or Fielding.

Miss Adela Quested

A young Englishwoman who comes to India with Mrs. Moore. She is expected to marry Mrs. Moore's son Ronny Heaslop, the Chandrapore city magistrate. Adela is a catalyst for the central dramatic events of the novel, and her behavior in these events radically affects the lives of the characters around her. Her accusation against Dr. Aziz, followed by her recantation during the trial, exposes the deep divisions between the British and Indians. On a more symbolic level, Adela may also be seen to represent most people's inability to communicate or to understand the deeper patterns and meaning of life.

Adela is described as "plain." (Because of her very plainness, Aziz is not at all attracted to her, and he is later insulted by the idea that anyone could think he would have wanted to rape her.) Although initially she is well-intentioned toward India, she does not possess Mrs. Moore's sensitivity and imagination. As a newcomer, she is somewhat naive about the nature of relations between the Anglo-Indians (British) and the Indians. Ronny expresses his disapproval of Adela's desire to see "the real India." While she is at Fielding's tea party, she offhandedly remarks that she is not planning to stay long in India. Immediately she—and the reader—realizes that unconsciously she has decided not to marry Ronny. However, she changes her mind temporarily when she and Ronny are in a minor accident in the Nawab Bahadur's car.

Adela accompanies Dr. Aziz and Mrs. Moore to the Marabar Caves. Here, while she is in one of the caves, something unexplained happens and she hurriedly runs out of the caves. Miss Derek, who happens along in her car, drives Adela back to Chandrapore, where Adela tells the authorities that Dr. Aziz had attempted to rape her. Ill and confused after her experience, Adela stays with the McBrydes before the trial. Although earlier Adela had not endeared herself to the British officials and their wives, they rally around her and denounce Aziz because she is "an English girl, fresh from

England." However, when she withdraws her charge against Aziz during the trial, she in effect renounces her own people. She breaks off her engagement with Ronny and stays with Fielding for a while before leaving India and returning to England. She does not reappear after this. However, in Part III, Dr. Aziz continues to harbor bad feelings toward her. He mistakenly believes that Fielding, who has also gone back to England, has married her—a misunderstanding that is not cleared up until just before the conclusion of the novel.

Mr. Turton

An Anglo-Indian (British) government administrator in Chandrapore. He holds the post of Collector, and is a generic representative of British authority in the district. Aziz uses the phrase "your Turtons and Burtons" to refer offhandedly to all British civil servants. Turton has been in India for twenty-five years, but his comments and actions show that he really does not understand the Indians. For example, he remarks that "India does wonders for the judgment, especially in hot weather." He organizes a "Bridge Party" so that Adela Quested and Mrs. Moore can meet some Indians. Although Turton is not particularly sensitive or imaginative, he is basically a decent man.

Mrs. Turton

The wife of the Collector at Chandrapore, Mr. Turton. She is a generic *memsahib*—the wife of an

Anglo-Indian (British) official. She is something of a snob. Mrs. Turton prefers to socialize with other British wives and their husbands in the tight-knit Anglo-Indian community and does not socialize with Indians except at formal events. She disapproves of Adela Quested.

Mr. Zulfiqar

See Nawab Bahadur

Themes

Culture Clash

At the heart of *A Passage to India*—and in the background—is a clash between two fundamentally different cultures, those of East and West. The British poet Rudyard Kipling, who was born in India and lived there for several years as an adult, wrote: "East is East and West is West, and never the twain shall meet." Without quoting or acknowledging Kipling, Forster adopts this premise as a central theme of *A Passage to India.*

The West is represented by the Anglo-Indians (the British administrators and their families in India) in Chandrapore. They form a relatively small but close-knit community. They live at the civil station, apart from the Indians. Their social life centers around the Chandrapore Club, where they attempt to recreate the entertainments that would be found in England. Although these Westerners wish to maintain good relations with the Easterners whom they govern, they have no desire to "understand" India or the Indians. Early in the book Ronny Heaslop remarks that "No one can even begin to think of knowing this country until he has been in it twenty years." When Adela Quested rebukes him for his attitudes, he replies that "India isn't home"—that is, it is not England.

Mrs. Moore, Adela, and Mr. Fielding are three

English characters who challenge this received wisdom. Significantly, Mrs. Moore and Adela are newcomers who have no experience of India and thus are not fully aware of the gulf that separates the two cultures: "They had no race-consciousness—Mrs. Moore was too old, Miss Quested too new—and they behaved to Aziz as to any young man who had been kind to them in the country." However, Adela shows her ignorance of Indian customs when she asks Dr. Aziz how many wives he has. The Turtons throw a "Bridge Party" to "bridge the gulf between East and West," but this event only emphasizes the awkwardness that exists between the two cultures. Mrs. Moore senses that India is full of "mystery and muddle" that Westerners cannot comprehend. Following Aziz's arrest, Turton tells Fielding that in his twenty-five years in India "I have never known anything but disaster result when English people and Indians attempt to be intimate socially."

The culture clash, however, is not only between Indians and Anglo-Indians, but also between two distinct groups of Indians—Moslems and Hindus. The narrative makes it clear that these two groups have very different traditions. Dr. Aziz is proud of his Moslem heritage and considers the Hindus to be almost alien. Hindus "have no idea of society," he tells Mrs. Moore, Adela, and Fielding. At the same time, although he is quite conscious of being an Indian, Aziz has a sentimental affection for Persia, the land from which Moslem culture originally spread to India. The Moslem-Hindu divide closes somewhat when a Hindu attorney, Mr.

Amritrao, is called in to defend Aziz. After the trial, Hindus and Moslems alike celebrate Aziz's acquittal. In the book's final section, Aziz is living in a Hindu state, where he regards himself as an outsider.

Friendship

E. M. Forster considered friendship to be one of the most important things in life. He once remarked, controversially, that if he were faced with the choice of betraying his country or betraying his friends, he would betray his country. *A Passage to India* explores the nature of friendship in its various forms, and the word "friend" occurs frequently throughout the book. When we first meet Dr. Aziz and his friends Hamidullah and Mahmoud Ali, they are discussing whether it is possible for Indians to be friends with the British. Hamidullah, who is pleasant and easygoing, fondly recalls his friendship with a British family long ago. When Dr. Aziz meets Mrs. Moore at the mosque, he feels she is someone with whom he can develop a friendship. He also wants to make friends with Cyril Fielding, whom he regards as a sympathetic and enlightened Englishman. However, despite his general impulsiveness, Aziz realizes that "a single meeting is too short to make a friend."

Aziz has a curious friendship with Professor Godbole. He likes Godbole but is unable to understand him. Godbole himself has a friendly attitude, but he is vague and distracted. When

Fielding tells him that Aziz has been arrested, Godbole seems unconcerned. Instead, he asks Fielding for advice about what name to give to a school that he is thinking of starting. Still, Fielding acknowledges that "all [Godbole's] friends trusted him, without knowing why."

Of all the British characters in the book, Fielding has the greatest gift for friendship. Mrs. Moore feels friendliness for Aziz when she first meets him, but she loses interest in friendship—and in life itself—when she loses her faith at the Marabar Caves. Among the other British characters, a sense of duty generally takes precedence over friendship. Although he had known her in England, Ronny is unable to sustain a relationship with Adela in India. In their words and actions, Anglo-Indian officials such as Ronny, Mr. Turton, and Mr. McBryde demonstrate that while they may get along with Indians on one level, it is impossible and indeed undesirable to be friends with them.

The book concludes with a conversation between Aziz and Fielding about the possibility of friendship—the theme that had been the subject of the first conversation. Aziz tells Fielding that they cannot be friends until the English have been driven out of India. Fielding replies that he wants to be friends, and that it is also what Aziz wants. The last paragraph, however, suggests that the impersonal forces at work in India will not yet allow such a friendship.

Public vs. Private Life

The various attempts at friendship throughout *A Passage to India* are frustrated not only by cultural differences but also by the demands of public life, or duty. These demands are strongest among the Anglo-Indian officials of Chandrapore. In general, characters such as Turton, Callendar, McBryde, and Ronny put their jobs above whatever personal desires they may have. The Turtons' "Bridge Party" is more a diplomatic exercise than a truly personal gesture. McBryde, the superintendent of police, prosecutes Aziz because it is his duty to do so; personal feelings do not enter into his decision. Ronny breaks off his engagement with Adela partly because her actions in the court are seen by the Anglo-Indians as a public disgrace. His marriage to her would offend the members of his community, who disapprove of Adela because of her behavior at the trial.

Cyril Fielding, the principal of the government college, seems to be the only British character willing to act out of personal conviction rather than public duty. The Anglo-Indian authorities believe it is important to keep up a public image of unity on the question of Aziz's guilt. In speaking up for Aziz, Fielding goes against the public behavior that is expected of him and is seen as "letting down the side." Because of this transgression, he is expelled from the English club at Chandrapore.

McBryde's affair with Miss Derek, revealed later in the book, is perhaps a minor instance in which another British official chooses to fulfill a personal desire at the risk of his public image. However, we do not see the consequences of this choice.

Dr. Aziz himself is torn between his public life as a doctor at a government hospital and his private dreams. When he attempts to transcend the distinction between private wishes and the public constraints, "Trouble after trouble encountered him, because he had challenged the spirit of the Indian earth, which tries to keep men in compartments." Only in Professor Godbole does the division between public and private life seem to disappear. For Godbole, the two are simply different forms of one existence. Godbole's prayers, for example, have both a private and public function, and it is difficult to tell where one ends and the other begins.

Topics for Further Study

- Research a specific aspect of life in

British India in the early twentieth century. Possible aspects for study include: the British colonial administration; the legal system; the Hindu caste system; the Native States and their relation to British India; Hindu-Moslem relations; the everyday lives of Anglo-Indian (British) families.

- Identify some of the various ethnic groups within India. In what regions do these people live? What languages do they speak, what religions do they practice, and what are some of their customs?

- Research Mohandas K. Gandhi and his philosophy of nonviolence and passive resistance. What were Gandhi's main beliefs and how did he practice them? What effect did his teachings and actions have?

Ambiguity

A Passage to India is full of ambiguity, and its most important characters—Dr. Aziz, Mrs. Moore, Cyril Fielding, Adela Quested—are beset by doubt at key points in the narrative. The terms "mystery" and "muddle" are introduced during Fielding's tea party and are repeated several times throughout the book. When Adela remarks that she "hates mysteries," Mrs. Moore replies that "I like mysteries but I rather dislike muddles." Mr. Fielding then observes that "a mystery is a muddle."

Doubt and ambiguity surround two key incidents in the book that occur at the Marabar Caves. On a literal level, Adela does not know if she has really been attacked in the cave or if she has only imagined this incident. If she has been attacked, was Dr. Aziz the attacker? While the reader might not doubt Aziz's innocence, there is a larger ambiguity about what really did take place. For Anglo-Indian authority figures such as Ronny Heaslop, Major Callendar, and Mr. McBryde, there is no doubt whatever; it is only characters such as Cyril Fielding who are capable of entertaining doubt and, thus, of thinking critically about events.

An even larger, more metaphorical ambiguity surrounds Mrs. Moore's experience at the caves. While she is inside one of the caves, she hears an echo and suddenly feels that everything—including her religious faith—is meaningless. So powerful is the doubt that fills Mrs. Moore, that she loses her grip on life.

God and Religion

E. M. Forster was not a religious man nor a religious writer. However, religion is a major preoccupation in the book. India is seen as a meeting point of three of the world's historic religions—Islam, Christianity, and Hinduism. Indeed, the three parts of the book—"Mosque,"

"Cave," and "Temple"—generally correspond to these religions. Aziz loves the cultural and social aspects of his Moslem (Islamic) heritage, but he seems less concerned with its theology and religious practice. He is aware that Moslems are in the minority in India, and he thus feels a special kinship with other Moslems such as Hamidullah. The Anglo-Indians are nominal representatives of Christianity, although there is little overt sign of such Christian virtues as charity, love, and forgiveness. Ronny Heaslop admits that for him Christianity is fine in its place, but he does not let it interfere with his civil duty. Mrs. Moore is basically Christian in her outlook. However, she experiences a crisis of faith during her visit to the Marabar Caves, and her belief in God or in any meaning to life is destroyed. Hinduism is the main religion of India, and Professor Godbole is the central Hindu figure in the book. He is also, by far, the most religious character. For Godbole, Hinduism is "completeness, not reconstruction." The central principle of this religion is the total acceptance of things as they are. Forster suggests that this is the most positive spiritual approach to life. It is also most representative of the true spirit of India.

Style

Point of View

A Passage to India is written in the third person, with an impersonal narrative voice. This technique makes the narrative seem traditional and straightforward, especially when compared to the more obviously experimental narrative techniques that were being used at the time by such novelists as James Joyce and Virginia Woolf. The narrator here is apparently omniscient, telling the reader much about India at the same time as describing the situations in which the various characters find themselves. At the same time, however, the narrative withholds a full explanation of certain events, most notably the misadventures that befall Mrs. Moore and Adela Quested at the Marabar Caves. Indeed, in recounting these details, the narrator is ambiguous rather than omniscient. A degree of ambiguity also surrounds the depiction of certain characters. Often, relatively minor characters (such as Mr. Turton, Mrs. Callendar, Mahmoud Ali, and the Nawab Bahadur) will appear in a scene without much introduction. Forster seems to take their presence for granted. This technique mimics the way that people might come and go in real life. Forster also assumes that the reader will have some knowledge of the social nuances of British India.

At times, the narrative focus shifts from a

depiction of external events and enters the consciousness of one character or another, almost without the reader noticing that such a shift has occurred. This stream-of-consciousness effect is evident when Forster writes about Mrs. Moore's experiences at the caves and when he reports Adela's perceptions during the trial. It is also used several times when the narrative records Aziz's thoughts about his Islamic heritage and about his place in India.

Setting

The action of the first two sections of the book takes place in the town of Chandrapore and at the Marabar Caves, located outside the town. Within the town itself, which is fairly nondescript, Forster identifies several localized settings. When we see the Anglo-Indian officials such as Major Callendar and Mr. Turton and their wives, it is almost invariably at the Civil Station, the area where the Anglo-Indians live and work. Often they are at the Chandrapore Club, which is exclusively for the Anglo-Indians and their British guests such as Mrs. Moore, and which Indians cannot enter. Although this setting emphasizes the Anglo-Indian's superior social status, it also shows their isolation from the mass of Indians who live around them. By contrast, the Indians are often shown at their own homes or in public places. The third section is set in Mau, a Hindu state several hundred miles from Chandrapore. (The book's three section headings —"Mosque," "Caves," and "Temple"—indicate the symbolic settings; see "Structure" and "Symbolism," below.)

Apart from these specific settings, India itself is the larger setting of the book. Indeed, some critics have remarked that India is not only the setting: it is also the subject and might even be considered a "character."

Critics have argued about the extent to which *A Passage to India* reflects actual historical and political conditions of the time in which it is set. Indeed, there is some critical dispute over exactly when the novel takes place; Forster gives no dates in the narrative. One Indian who admired the book believed that it was more representative of India at the time of Forster's first visit, 1912. Several Western critics have agreed with this analysis, and one has claimed that the action of the novel occurs "out of time." It may be safe to assume that the time setting is an amalgamation of the early 1910s and the early 1920s.

Structure

A Passage to India is divided into three parts or sections. Each part has its own particular symbols, correspondences, and associations. Each is set in a different season and opens with a chapter that describes a particular aspect of India. Part I, titled "Mosque," takes place during the cool, dry season. The Mosque where Dr. Aziz meets Mrs. Moore corresponds to Islam and the Islamic or Moslem aspect of India, as represented by Dr. Aziz and his family and friends. Despite some hints of possible trouble, the prevailing mood is one of harmony. The main events of this part of the book are Aziz's meeting with Mrs. Moore and Mr. Fielding's tea party.

Part II, "Caves," takes place during the hot season. The focus shifts to the British domination of India and to a contemporary British Christian perspective. Adela Quested becomes the center of attention. This part of the novel is marked by misunderstanding and conflict (or mystery and muddle, to use Mrs. Moore's earlier terms). Mrs. Moore gives in to despair after she hears the echo while she is in the cave, and Adela becomes completely confused. The incident at the Marabar Caves and the trial of Dr. Aziz make up the main dramatic action.

Part III, "Temple," takes place during the rainy season several years after the action of Parts I and II. Dr. Aziz has settled in a Hindu state, Mau. Professor Godbole becomes a more prominent character. This part of the novel concentrates on the themes of rebirth and reconciliation. The primary events are the Hindu festival celebrating the rebirth of Krishna and Fielding's return to India. Part III is the shortest of the three sections of the novel and might be considered as an epilogue.

Motif

Just as the three-part structure gives the novel dramatic shape, the use of certain motifs helps to give the book dramatic unity. A *motif is* a recurring image or incident that has a suggestive and even a symbolic quality. One prominent motif in *A Passage to India* is the interrupted or delayed journey. This first occurs in chapter two, when Dr. Aziz is riding his bicycle to Major Callendar's bungalow at the English civil station and gets a flat tire. He has to find a tonga, or carriage, to take him the rest of the way. By the time he finally arrives, the major has left. Aziz's failure to arrive on time suggests the wide gulf that separates the Indians and the British. (To make matters worse, two English ladies appear and take Aziz's carriage, leaving him without transportation.)

Another interrupted journey is the ride that Adela and Ronny take in the Nawab Bahadur's car. There is a minor accident—in the darkness the car runs off the road, stranding the passengers until Miss Derek comes along and offers to take them back to Chandrapore in her car. (But she leaves the Nawab's chauffeur behind.) During this episode, Adela and Ronny decide that they will marry after all; but their engagement will prove to be temporary. This interrupted journey suggests their failure to marry.

In Part II of the novel, Cyril Fielding and Professor Godbole miss the train that they are intending to take on the trip to the Marabar Caves. This failure separates them from Aziz, Mrs. Moore, and Adela, who go on without them. The reader is left to imagine that if Fielding and Godbole had been able to accompany Aziz and the women as they had planned, the terrible and confusing incidents that befall the members of the party at the Marabar Caves might never have occurred. Later, Mrs. Moore dies on her voyage back to England.

In the final section, as they travel to the native state of Mau where Aziz and Godbole are living, Fielding, Stella, and Ralph are delayed by floods caused by the monsoons. Just before the end of the book, Aziz takes Ralph out on the river in a boat ("a rudderless dingy"); the oars had been "hidden to deter the visitors from going out." Fielding and his wife have already gone out in another boat, using long poles to push themselves. Aziz fears that the couple "might get into difficulties, for the wind was rising." The two boats collide and the passengers spill into the river. Despite the accident, this time the journey ends safely. The four characters have witnessed the Hindu celebrations, and their immersion in the water suggests not drowning but rebirth and renewal.

Irony

E. M. Forster has been called an ironic writer, and *A Passage to India* is perhaps the most ironic of all his works. Several layers of irony are evident. For example, it is ironic that Aziz has organized the trip to the Marabar Caves in order to entertain his English guests. Rather than being the pleasant outing that Aziz intended, the excursion ends in disaster for everyone concerned. Something happens to Adela while she is in one of the caves:

she believes that she has been attacked by Aziz. Aziz, who had prided himself on his hospitality, instead finds himself punished for a crime he did not commit. (There is also a minor irony in that Aziz finds Adela physically unattractive and is offended that anyone could think that he would want to rape her.) Mrs. Moore too suffers a fate more terrible than Adela's. While she is in the cave she hears an echo that is simply a meaningless noise—"ouboum." She takes this to mean that everything is meaningless, and thus she loses her faith. It is also ironic that, although the caves are reputed to be famous, there is really nothing remarkable about them except their effect on the visitors.

A further irony occurs later in the book when Dr. Aziz assumes that his friend Cyril Fielding has married Adela Quested. In fact, Fielding has married Stella Moore, the daughter of the late Mrs. Moore, whom Aziz greatly liked and admired. Also ironic is the suggestion that Stella, who has just arrived from England, may have a greater understanding of the mystery of India than does Aziz himself.

Symbolism

Although *A Passage to India* is a realistic novel, it also contains many symbolic elements. The most obvious symbols are those that give the titles of the book's three sections—mosque, cave, and temple. Both for Aziz and Mrs. Moore, the mosque is a symbol of refuge and peace, a place of sanctuary. The first meeting of Aziz and Mrs. Moore takes place in the mosque at night, under the moonlight. Mrs. Moore has gone to the mosque because she is bored with the play she has been attending at the Chandrapore club. The English play, *Cousin Kate*, seems artificial and out of place in India. The mosque, by contrast, is one symbol of the "real" India.

The cave bears some resemblance to the mosque, in that both are enclosed spaces. Here, however, the resemblance ends. The cave is dark, featureless, and menacing. Although there are many caves at Marabar, it is impossible to tell one from another; they are all alike. Critics have argued about the symbolic meaning of the cave. It is at least certain that whatever else they might suggest, they stand for misunderstanding and meaninglessness, or what Mrs. Moore calls "muddle."

Prominent among other symbols is the wasp. When Mrs. Moore goes to hang up her cloak at the end of chapter three, she sees a wasp. The symbolic significance of the wasp is not spelled out. However, it suggests the natural life of India, and also carries a hint of uncertainty. Much later, in Part III, Professor Godbole recalls "an old woman he had met in Chandrapore days." He then remembers "a wasp seen he forgot where.... He loved the wasp equally...."

Historical Context

Forster's England

Although the action of *A Passage to India* takes place entirely in India, it should be remembered that Forster was a British writer, and that most of his readers were British. Thus, the work reflects not only the contemporary India, which is its overt subject, but also England and the milieu in which Forster lived and wrote. Moreover, although Forster published the book in 1924 during the reign of King George V (r. 1910-36), he is commonly regarded as an Edwardian novelist. Forster's first four novels were written in the first decade of the twentieth century, during the reign of King Edward VII (r. 1901-10), and his values and outlook were developed during this period, before World War I. Thus, like Forster's earlier books, *A Passage to India* is commonly regarded as an Edwardian book (an Edwardian novel of manners, at that), even though it was not written during the Edwardian period.

Between the time Forster first visited India and began writing this novel (1912-13) and the time he finished it (1924), Britain had undergone the traumatic experience of World War I. Britain and hei allies won the war, but more than 750,000 British soldiers were killed, along with another quarter ol a million soldiers from other parts of the

British Empire; another two million British and Empire soldiers were wounded, many of them severely. These losses affected people's attitudes toward tradition and authority. The self-confidence that earlier had marked Britain's attitude about its empire and its place in the world was replaced with doubt and uncertainty. Nonetheless, although there was some sympathy for the Indian cause, most British people at the time would have supported the British presence in India.

Between 1912 and 1924, the British political landscape had also changed. At the beginning of this period, the Liberal Party had been one of the two major parties in Britain. (The other major party was, and remains, the Conservative Party.) The Liberals had won the majority of votes in the election of 1908, and were in power from that time until 1915. However, during this decade the Liberals lost much of their support to the newer and more radical Labour Party, which favored a socialist program. The Labour Party had its first election victory in 1924; by this time, the Liberal Party had dwindled to a third-party status, and it never won another general election. (Forster and most of his circle, including the members of the Bloomsbury Group, were Labour supporters.) Although Labour remained in power for only ten months in 1924, the party had become the main alternative to the Conservatives.

During this period the British Empire was beginning to change. This change was most evident in Ireland, the only region of the British Empire that was right on Britain's doorstep. On Easter Sunday, 1916, a group of Irish rebels declared Irish independence from Britain and attempted to seize control of Dublin. Although the British army quickly crushed the rebellion, a more widespread Irish independence movement soon arose, and in 1921 the British government signed a treaty recognizing self-rule for the twenty-six southern counties of Ireland.

The Indian Context

Although the Irish rebellion had no direct effect on British rule of India, the fact that Ireland had gained limited independence helped to strengthen the idea of possible Indian independence in the minds of many Indians. Forster's novel is set during a time of increased tension between the British and their Indian subjects. The British presence in India had begun in the 1600s, when a British trading company, the East India Company, gained a strong foothold in Madras, Bombay, and Calcutta. At this time, much of India was nominally governed by a royal Moslem dynasty, the Moguls. (It was the Mogul emperors and their court that Dr. Aziz in the novel idealized.) However, the Mogul government was weakened by infighting and was unable to control all of India. The Indian population consisted of a number of different ethnic and religious groups, with little sense of an overall Indian identity. The British were thus able to increase their power in India.

Compare & Contrast

- **1910s-1920s:** The British Empire stretches around the world. British-ruled territory in Asia includes present-day India, Pakistan, Bangladesh, Burma, Malaysia, and Singapore. Such present-day African countries as Egypt, Nigeria, Kenya, Zimbabwe, and South Africa are also part of the Empire, as are many Caribbean islands.

  Today: Virtually all the former British colonies are independent nations. Many retain loose trade and cultural ties with Britain in an association called the Commonwealth of Nations. Hong Kong, one of the last remaining British crown colonies, returned to Chinese rule at midnight on June 30, 1997.

- **1910s-1920s:** Britain is a major world power with a large industrial base and dominates international trade. Much of the raw material for Britain's manufacturers comes from India and other British colonies.

  Today: Britain is a small nation with a largely service-based economy. It is a member of the European Union (formerly the

European Economic Community), a close economic association of European nations. Britain trades widely with other European nations in the EU. After a period of economic change that saw the decline of traditional industries such as mining, manufacturing, and shipbuilding, Britain is now one of the most prosperous nations in Europe. Foreign-owned businesses operate successfully in Britain.

- **1910s-1920s:** The population of Britain is comprised almost entirely of English, Scottish, and Welsh people. A small number of elite students from India and other parts of the Empire are educated at British universities.

   Today: Immigrants from former colonies, and their descendants, make up approximately five percent of the British population. Some large British cities, including London, have substantial Indian, Pakistani, and Bangladeshi communities.

- **1910s-1920s:** Mohandas K. Gandhi, an Indian lawyer educated in Britain, develops his philosophy of passive resistance to British rule. By 1920 he has become a leading figure in the Indian National Congress, a political and cultural organization that works for fair treatment and increased civil rights for Indians. Support for independence grows.

Today: India (predominantly Hindu) and Pakistan (Moslem), formed out of former British India, have been independent since 1947. The two nations have fought several wars against each other, and relations are peaceful but uneasy. There is also ethnic and political violence within both countries. In India, the Congress Party (the successor to the Indian National Congress) was the dominant political party until the 1990s. Among Hindus, Gandhi remains a revered historical figure.

In 1773, the English Parliament created the post of Governor General for India. Under Governor-General Cornwallis (1786-93), the British established a sophisticated colonial administration in India. (Cornwallis was also the British general who had surrendered to George Washington at the end of the American Revolutionary War.) Cornwallis instituted a system of British rule that was still mostly intact at the time of *A Passage to India.*

Indians were forbidden to hold high

government office and were subject to other laws that kept them in a subservient position, both legally and economically. A number of areas of the country —known as Native States or Independent States— were not under direct British rule, but were governed by local Indian princes or maharajahs. However, the British authorities kept close watch on these states, which had friendly policies toward the British.

The British suppressed an Indian rebellion (known as the Indian Mutiny or Sepoy Rebellion) in 1857. By the time of *A Passage to India*, there was a significant organized movement for Indian equality and eventual independence, in the form of the Indian National Congress. In 1919, nearly 400 Indians were shot to death and another 1,200 wounded when soldiers under British command opened fire on a crowd that had gathered illegally in the northeast Indian town of Amritsar. The Amritsar Massacre, as it became known, caused a public outcry both in India and Britain. India stood poised on the edge of widespread violence. In this tense atmosphere, a British-educated Indian lawyer named Mohandas K. Gandhi began a long nonviolent campaign of civil disobedience against British rule. Gandhi advocated Indian equality as well as peaceful cooperation between the country's Hindu and Moslem populations. Forster does not mention Gandhi or the Amritsar Massacre, but the division between India's Hindus and Moslems is a major concern in the novel.

There is some critical dispute over the time

period during which Forster's novel is set. One Indian who admired the book believed that it was representative of India at the time of Forster's first visit, 1912. One American critic has claimed that the action occurs "out of time." Most critics and readers feel that the action takes place in the early 1920s, contemporary with the time that the book was finished and published.

In any case, Forster's novel is not only concerned with its own time but also looks forward to the future. The novel hints that the two groups may be able to put aside their traditional differences and live in harmony as Indians. However, this did not turn out to be the case. As independence grew nearer, Moslems demanded the creation of a separate Moslem nation, Pakistan. Indian independence in 1947 was accompanied by violent clashes between Hindus and Moslems, with tens of thousands of deaths on both sides. The next year, Gandhi was assassinated by a Hindu fanatic who believed that Gandhi was making too many compromises with the Moslems. Ironically, today both India and Pakistan have relatively good relations with Britain and the British. So it is likely that Dr. Aziz and Mr. Fielding would today be able to have the sort of uninhibited friendship that is mentioned at the end of the book.

Critical Overview

When *A Passage to India* was published in 1924, E. M. Forster was already a well-known and highly respected novelist. However, he had not published a novel for fourteen years *(Howards End,* 1910, was his previous book). Upon its publication, *A Passage to India* was reviewed widely in British newspapers and literary journals, as well as in American magazines. Most of these early reviews were very favorable and helped to ensure the book's success.

Among the first reviewers of *A Passage to India* in Britain and America were the English novelists Rose Macaulay *(Daily News,* June 4, 1924) and L. P. Hartley *(The Spectator,* June 28, 1924); the British writer and publisher Leonard Woolf *(The Nation and Atheneum,* June 14, 1924); and the Scottish poet Edwin Muir *(The Nation,* October 8, 1924). All of these reviews were positive; in fact, these writers believed that *A Passage to India* was the best novel that Forster had written. A review in the London *Times Literary Supplement* concluded that Forster "portrays the super-sensitiveness, the impulsiveness, the charm and the weakness, of Mohammedan and Hindu India, in order to emphasize the honesty, the arrogance ... and the moral tremors of the governing caste." In the United States, Robert Morss Lovett wrote a favorable review in *The New Republic* (August 16, 1924). However, E. A. Home in *The New Statesman* in London criticized Forster for his unsympathetic portrayal of the book's Anglo-Indian (British) characters and pointed out some inaccuracies in Forster's depiction of India.

Two of Forster's distinguished contemporaries expressed differing views of *A Passage to India* in personal remarks. The celebrated military hero T. E. Lawrence—Lawrence of Arabia—told Forster that *A Passage to India* was "universal: the bitter hopeless picture a cloud might have painted, of man in India." However, the novelist D. H. Lawrence (no relation to T. E. Lawrence) commented that the book was filled with "people, people, and nothing but people."

In the decades since its publication, *A Passage to India* has continued to receive close and respectful attention from many distinguished scholars and critics, often as part of a consideration of Forster's writing in general. With her husband Leonard, Virginia Woolf was an early—though not entirely uncritical—supporter of Forster's work. She discussed the book in a 1927 essay, "The Novels of E. M. Forster," in the *Atlantic Monthly.* Rose Macaulay, who like Forster was a graduate of Cambridge University, wrote one of the first full-length books about Forster, *The Writings of E. M. Forster*, published in 1938. That same year the influential English critic F. R. Leavis wrote about Forster in his Cambridge journal, *Scrutiny.* The famous American critic Lionel Trilling discussed *A Passage to India* in 1943 in *E. M. Forster: A Study*, thereby helping to revive American interest in the work nearly twenty years after its publication.

More recent academic studies in both Britain and America have focused attention on particular aspects of Forster's book, such as its narrative technique, symbolism, and politics. Malcolm Bradbury and Jeffrey Meyers are among those who have made important contributions to scholarship on *A Passage to India.*

Sources

Parminder Bakshi, "The Politics of Desire: E. M. Forster's Encounters with India," in *A Passage to India: Theory and Practice Series*, edited by Tony Davies and Nigel Wood, Open University Press, 1994, pp. 23-64.

Benita Parry, "The Politics of Representation in ¢ Passage to India, '" in *E. M. Forster: Contemporary Critical Essays*, edited by Jeremy Tambling, MacMillan (London), 1994, pp. 133-50.

Review of *A Passage to India*, in *Times Literary Supplement*, June 12, 1924, p. 37.

Jenny Sharpe, "The Unspeakable Limits of Rape: Colonial Violence and Counter-Insurgency," in *Genders*, No. 10, Spring, 1991, pp. 25-46.

For Further Study

Malcolm Bradbury, "Two Passages to India: Forster as Victorian and Modern," in *Aspects of E. M. Forster*, edited by Oliver Stallybrass, London, 1969, pp. 124-25.

> Bradbury sees Forster as "a central figure of the transition into modernism."

Tony Davies, "Introduction," in *A Passage to India: Theory and Practice Series*, edited by Tony Davies and Nigel Wood, Open University Press, 1994, pp. 1-22.

> Davies discusses critical commentary on *A Passage to India*, from early reviews to contemporary analysis.

Philip Gardner, "E. M. Forster" in *British Writers, Vol. VI: Thomas Hardy to Wilfred Owen*, General Editor Ina Scott-Kilvert, The British Council and Charles Scribner's Sons, 1983, pp. 397-413.

> Gardner identifies and analyzes several levels on which the action of the novel moves, with special attention to the symbolic element.

Philip Gardner, *E. M. Forster: The Critical Heritage*, Routlege & Kegan Paul, 1973.

> A good survey of critical interpretations of and reactions to the

works of Forster up to the early 1970s.

Francis King, *E. M. Forster*, Thames & Hudson, 1988.

> This copiously illustrated biography in Thames and Hudson's popular "Literary Lives" series provides an engaging introduction to Forster's life and work. King discusses Forster's writing of *A Passage to India* in the context of the author's travels and concerns. For general readers.

Stephen K. Land, "A Passage to India," in *Challenge and Conventionality in the Fiction of E. M. Forster*, AMS Press, 1990, pp. 189-217.

> Land's chapter on *A Passage to India* touches on many of the major issues in the novel and makes frequent comparisons to Forster's other works.

F. R. Leavis, "E. M. Forster," in *Scrutiny*, No. 7, September, 1938, pp. 188-202.

> An essay by the influential British critic that helped to canonize Forster as a major twentieth-century novelist.

Rose Macaulay, *The Writings of E. M. Forster*, London, 1938.

James McConkey, *The Novels of E. M. Forster*, Cornell University Press, 1957.

McConkey's book remains valuable both for its close study of Forster's novels in general and for its perceptive and useful discussion of *A Passage to India* Frederick P. W. McDowell, "E. M. Forster," in *Dictionary of Literary Biography, Vol. 34: British Novelists, 1890-1929: Traditionalists*, edited by Thomas F. Staley, Gale Re-search Company, 1985, pp. 121-51.

A survey of Forster's life and works, with a thorough synopsis of *A Passage to India* and a discussion of the book's symbolism.

Jeffrey Meyers, "The Politics of A *Passage to India,"* in *Journal of Modern Literature*, Vol. 1, No. 3, March, 1971, pp. 329-38.

> Meyers calls attention to the political and historical references of *A Passage to India*, which he believes have been ignored or underestimated by previous critics.

Leland Monk, "Apropos of Nothing: Chance and Narrative in Forster's ¢ Passage to India,'" in *Studies in the Novel*, Vol. 26, No. 4, 1994, pp. 392-403.

> Monk examines the narrative techniques of each of the novel's three sections and contends that the third is concerned with the importance of chance.

Judith Ruderman, "E. M. Forster" in *Encyclopedia of World Literature in the 20th Century*, revised edition, Vol. 2, General Editor Leonard S. Klein, Continuum Publishing Company/Frederick Ungar Publishing, 1982, pp. 121-25.

> Ruderman notes that Forster's novels move from speech into silence, and that in *A Passage to India* Forster "recognizes the limits of the humanistic creed" and suggests that "human intercourse may be impossible and language in vain."

Chaman L. Sahni, *E. M. Forster's Passages to India: The Religious Dimension*, Heinemann, 1981.

> A study of Moslem-Hindu relations in the novel and the book's representation of religion and religious symbolism.

Wilfred Stone, *The Cave and the Mountain: A Study of E. M. Forster*, Stanford University Press, 1966.

> A book-length analysis of all Forster's novels. Stone regards Forster as not only a liberal humanist but also a visionary prophet akin to D. H. Lawrence. In Stone's interpretation, the cave in *A Passage to India* is a symbol of the "underworld of human experience."

Virginia Woolf, "The Novels of E. M. Forster," *Atlantic Monthly*, Vol. 115, No. 5, November, 1927;

reprinted in Woolf's *The Death of the Moth and Other Essays*, London, 1942, and in *E. M. Forster: The Critical Heritage*, edited by Philip Gardner, Boston and London, 1973, pp. 321-24.

> An early assessment of Forster's output by one of his leading contemporaries. Novelist Woolf notes Forster's similarity to Jane Austen in the way he captures "the shades and shadows of the social comedy," but she finds that in *A Passage to India* the realistic and symbolic aspects of Forster's narrative technique do not mesh successfully.

Lightning Source UK Ltd.
Milton Keynes UK
UKHW020755150822
407319UK00012B/2292